Tax Gap, Tax Compliance, and Proposed Legislation in the 112th Congress

James M. Bickley
Specialist in Public Finance

September 20, 2012

Congressional Research Service

7-5700

www.crs.gov

R42739

CRS Report for Congress
Prepared for Members and Committees of Congress

Summary

Recent and projected large federal budget deficits and the need for revenue offsets under the Pay-As-You-Go Act (PAYGO) have generated congressional interest in the feasibility of increasing revenue by reducing the tax gap. The Internal Revenue Service (IRS) defines the *gross* tax gap as the difference between the tax liability imposed by law for a given tax year and the amount of tax that taxpayers pay *voluntarily* and on time for that year. It defines the *net* tax gap as the amount of the gross tax gap that remains unpaid after all enforced and other late payments are made for the tax year. For tax (calendar) year 2006 (the most recent year for which data are available), the IRS estimated a gross tax gap of $450 billion, equal to a noncompliance rate of 16.9%. For the same tax year, IRS enforcement activities, coupled with other late payments, recovered about $65 billion of the gross tax gap, resulting in an estimated net tax gap of $385 billion.

The estimated gross tax gap of $450 billion consisted of underreporting of tax liability ($376 billion), nonfiling of tax returns ($28 billion), and underpayment of taxes ($46 billion). (Taxes on illegal activities are excluded from these estimates.) Most of the underreporting of tax liability concerned underreporting of individual income liability ($235 billion). The percentage of individual income that was underreported varied significantly depending on the degree of information reporting and whether or not withholding was required. For the 2006 tax gap estimate, the IRS primarily utilized data from the National Research Program (NRP), which seeks to obtain the optimal balance among research quality, efficiency, and the reduction of taxpayer burden.

Estimates of the gross tax gap have been heavily publicized; perhaps as a result, some public officials have emphasized better enforcement of tax laws in order to raise revenue. Three factors affect the dollar amount that can be collected by increased enforcement: some types of unreported income are difficult to detect, some of the detected tax liability cannot be easily collected, and many detected tax liabilities are small relative to enforcement costs.

From FY2001 to FY2011, enforcement revenues collected by the IRS increased from $33.8 billion to $55.2 billion. Also from FY2001 to FY2011, IRS staffing for key enforcement occupations rose from 20,203 to 22,184.

Over the past four years, the IRS has focused on six strategy priorities: technology modernization, tax return preparers, data analytics, taxpayer service, offshore tax evasion, and workforce job satisfaction. The pursuit of most of these priorities reduces the tax gap. The IRS has put in place the major facets of its tax return preparer initiative.

 In the 112ᵗʰ Congress, legislation concerning tax compliance has been introduced in the following seven areas: repeal of the 1099 reporting requirement (H.R. 4); identity theft (S. 1534, S. 3432, H.R. 3215, H.R. 3482, and H.R. 6205); free file (S. 1796 and H.R. 2569); contracting (H.R. 829); insurance companies (S. 1693 and H.R. 3157); tax havens (S. 1346, H.R. 2669, S. 2075, and H.R. 3338); and tax avoidance by expatriates (S. 3205).

This report will be updated as issues develop or new legislation is introduced.

Contents

Figures

Tables

Appendixes

Contacts

Introduction

Recent and projected large federal budget deficits have generated congressional and executive branch interest in increasing revenue by reducing the tax gap.[1] Specific methods for lowering the tax gap may also be used as revenue offsets under the Pay-As-You-Go Act (PAYGO).[2] Other motivations for reducing the tax gap include adverse effects on (1) public trust in the fairness of the tax system, which may adversely affect voluntary compliance with tax laws, and (2) economic efficiency, by providing an incentive for inputs of labor and capital to shift to those sectors of the economy with greater opportunities to evade taxes.[3]

This report defines tax gap concepts, explains the methodology used to estimate the tax gap, discusses the relationship between the tax gap and enforcement, explains the Internal Revenue Service's (IRS's) strategic priorities, examines the IRS return preparer initiative, and describes proposed legislation in the 112ᵗʰ Congress.

Tax Gap Concepts

The IRS has defined the concepts of a gross tax gap and a net tax gap. The IRS defines the *gross* tax gap as the difference between the aggregate tax liability imposed by law for a given tax year and the amount of tax that taxpayers pay *voluntarily* and on time for that year.[4] And it defines the *net* tax gap as the amount of the gross tax gap that remains unpaid after all enforced and other late payments are made for the tax year.[5] Also, the net tax gap is measured after any subsequent appeals and litigation; consequently, this measurement is more accurate a number of years after the taxes were due.[6]

Currently, the measurements of these tax gap concepts exclude illegal activities because the IRS lacks adequate data on these activities. Also, the IRS does not currently include the international tax gap. The Treasury Inspector General for Tax Administration has reported that known estimates of the total international tax gap range from a low of $42.8 billion to a high of $123.0 billion.[7]

---

[1] For the current outlook on the federal budget, see U.S. Congressional Budget Office, *An Update to the Budget and Economic Outlook: Fiscal Years 2012 to 2022*, August 2012.

[2] For information about PAYGO, see CRS Report R41157, *The Statutory Pay-As-You-Go Act of 2010: Summary and Legislative History*, by Bill Heniff Jr.

[3] For a comprehensive review of the literature on tax compliance, see James Adreoni, Brian Erard, and Jonathan Feinstein, "Tax Compliance," *Journal of Economic Literature*, vol. 36, no. 2, June 1998, pp. 818-860. For an overview of the economics of tax evasion, see Joel Slemrod, "Cheating Ourselves: The Economics of Tax Evasion," *Journal of Economic Perspectives*, vol. 21, no. 1, winter 2007, pp. 25-48.

[4] U.S. Department of the Treasury, Internal Revenue Service, *Reducing the Federal Tax Gap: A Report on Improving Voluntary Compliance*, August 2, 2007, p. 6.

[5] Ibid., pp. 9-10.

[6] U.S. General Accounting Office, *Taxpayer Compliance: Analyzing the Nature of the Income Tax Gap*, Statement of Lynda D. Willis, Director, Tax Policy and Administration Issues, General Government Division, before the National Commission on Restructuring the Internal Revenue Service, GAO/T-GGD-97-35, January 9, 1997, p. 3.

[7] U.S. Department of the Treasury, Treasury Inspector General for Tax Administration, *A Combination of Legislative Actions and Increased IRS Capacity are Required to Reduce the Multi-Billion Dollar U.S. International Tax Gap*, report reference number 2009-IE-R001, January 27, 2009, p. 19.

For tax year 2006 (the most recent year for which data are available), the IRS estimated a gross tax gap of $450 billion, equal to a voluntary compliance rate (VCR) of 83.1%.[8] For the same year, IRS enforcement activities, coupled with other late payments, recovered about $65 billion of the gross tax gap, resulting in an estimated net tax gap of $385 billion.[9]

The estimated gross tax gap of $450 billion consisted of underreporting of tax liability ($376 billion), nonfiling of tax returns ($28 billion), and underpayment of taxes ($46 billion).[10] For 2006, the $376 billion of underreporting of tax liability had the following components: $235 billion in individual income tax, $67 billion in corporate income tax, $72 billion in employment tax, and $2 billion in estate taxes.[11] There was no estimate of the underreporting of excise taxes.[12]

The percentage of individual income tax that was underreported varied significantly depending on the degree of information reporting and whether or not withholding was required.[13] For example, in 2006, 1% of the taxes on the sum of wages, salaries, and tips was underreported because of substantial information reporting and withholding.[14] But 56% of the total of nonfarm proprietor income, other income, rents and royalties, farm income, and income on Form 4797 (sales of business property) was underreported due to little or no information reporting.[15] These data indicate that increased information reporting and withholding would reduce the tax gap. The increased revenue would have to be weighed against higher administrative costs of the IRS and higher compliance costs of individuals.

Methodology to Estimate the Tax Gap

Since taxpayers do not report their underreporting of tax liability, the IRS has utilized evolving methods to estimate the tax gap. Prior to 1989, it used the Taxpayer Compliance Measurement Program (TCMP). Currently, the IRS utilizes the National Research Program (NRP) to estimate the gross income tax gap.[16]

Taxpayer Compliance Measurement Program

Prior to tax year 1989, the IRS relied on data from the TCMP to estimate the gross tax gap for individual income taxpayers and small corporations (less than $10 million in assets). The IRS formulated upper- and lower-bound estimates of the gross income tax gap. The IRS completed

---

[8] The VCR is defined as 1 minus the ratio of the gross tax gap to total liabilities. U.S. Department of the Treasury, Internal Revenue Service, *Tax Gap for Tax Year 2006: Overview*, January 6, 2012, p. 1.

[9] U. S. Department of the Treasury, Internal Revenue Service, *Tax Gap "Map,"* December 2011.This reference is shown in **Figure A-1** in **Appendix A**.

[10] Ibid.

[11] Ibid.

[12] Ibid.

[13] U.S. Department of the Treasury, Internal Revenue Service, *Effect of Information Reporting on Taxpayer Compliance*, 2006, December 2011. This reference is shown in **Figure A-2** in **Appendix A**.

[14] Ibid.

[15] Ibid.

[16] These methodologies to estimate the tax gap are examined in detail in the following source: Eric Toder, "What is the Tax Gap?" *Tax Notes*, October 22, 2007, pp. 367-388.

"line-by-line examinations of several different types of tax returns."[17] The upper-bound estimates of the gross tax gap were calculated from the TCMP and regular audits of large corporations. For larger corporations ($10 million or more in assets), the IRS relied on regular operational audits of tax returns. If an audit showed an underpayment of taxes, the IRS examiner determined the tax deficiency.[18]

The lower-bound estimate of the gross tax gap was based on the amounts eventually assessed after the appeals and litigation process. Some of the tax deficiency found from audits was negated by taxpayers' appeals and court decisions leading to a lower estimate of taxes owed but unpaid.[19] "The eventual assessment may be considered to be the true 'legal' liability in the sense that IRS cannot attempt to assess more later, except in unusual cases."[20] The net tax gap differed depending on whether the upper- or lower-bound estimate of the gross tax gap was used.

National Research Program

The last TCMP was for tax year 1988. Several times in the 1990s, IRS officials attempted to conduct a new TCMP, but some members of Congress objected because of the high cost to the IRS and the compliance burden placed on taxpayers who were selected in the TCMP sample. Consequently, IRS developed the National Research Program. According to the IRS,

> The NRP approach to measuring reporting compliance balances research quality, efficiency and the reduction of taxpayer burden. It establishes a tax return sample that is representative of the individual taxpayer population. NRP focuses on obtaining reliable data in the most cost-effective manner possible by using innovative and efficient techniques that maintain taxpayer rights to privacy.[21]

The NRP was used in estimating the 2001 and 2006 tax gaps. The 2006 tax gap estimates "are based on a variety of data sources and methodologies."[22] The primary source was the NRP for 2006.

> The IRS studied individual taxpayer compliance through the NRP and used the resulting compliance data to estimate the tax gap for individual income tax underreporting and the portion of employment tax underreporting attributed to self-employment taxes for tax year 2006.
>
> The 2006 individual NRP involved auditing a random selection of about 13,000 to 14,000 individual tax returns.... Starting with the 2006 individual NRP compliance study, IRS is using a rolling sample, which will combine samples across three years. According to the IRS, this change will reduce cost and provide more up to date compliance data. The sample

---

[17] Internal Revenue Service, *Income Tax Compliance Research: Net Tax Gap and Remittance Gap Estimates* (Washington, April 1990), p. 2.

[18] Ibid., p. 13.

[19] Ibid., pp. 13-14.

[20] Ibid., p. 14.

[21] U.S. Treasury, Internal Revenue Service, *Internal Revenue Service Manual – NRP Overview*, Chapter 22, Section 1, April 25, 2008.

[22] U.S. Government Accountability Office, *Tax Gap: Sources of Noncompliance and Strategies to Reduce It*, Statement of James R. White, Director Strategic Issues, before the U.S. Congress, House Committee on Oversight and Government Reform, GAO-12-651T, April 19, 2012, p. 16.

design for the 2006 individual NRP included 11 primary strata, which were based on the examination classes used in audit workload selection. Also the 2006 individual NRP was designed to oversample returns with business income reported on Schedules C, E, or F or Form 2106.[23]

Tax Enforcement

The estimates of the gross tax gap have been heavily publicized. Perhaps as a result, some public officials have emphasized better enforcement of tax laws to increase revenue. According to some, enforcement alone is likely to have a limited impact on the gross tax gap. Acting on this view, the IRS is implementing what it terms a comprehensive approach to reduce the gross tax gap.

Limitations to Increased Enforcement

Three factors are seen as limiting the net revenue potential from increased enforcement. First, much of the gross tax gap for individual income tax filers is due to types of unreported income that are difficult to detect. Usually the income is not covered by third-party information returns (e.g., income earned by informal business proprietors who operate on a cash basis). Second, even when the unreported income is detected, some of the resulting tax liability cannot be easily collected, particularly from those taxpayers who are currently unable to pay. Third, many detected tax liabilities are so small relative to enforcement costs that it is not seen as cost effective to pursue collection.

Tax Enforcement Efforts FY2001-FY2011

Some analysts contend that empirical data suggest that additional tax enforcement actions alone would have a limited effect on the gross tax gap.

From FY2001 to FY2011, greater tax enforcement efforts by the IRS increased enforcement revenue from $33.8 billion to $55.2 billion.[24] While $21.4 billion represents a 63.3% increase, it is 6.2% of the estimated $345 billion gross tax gap in 2001. During the period FY2001-FY2007, staffing for key enforcement occupations rose from 20,113 to 21,187 (5.3%); examinations of individual tax returns increased from 731,756 (or 0.58% of returns) to 1,384,563 (or 1.03% of returns); examinations of business returns rose from 7,384,600 (or 0.55% of returns) to 9,072,828 (or 0.66% of returns); and examinations of tax-exempt organization returns increased from 5,342 (or 0.61% of returns) to 7,580 (or 0.87% of returns).[25]

For FY2008, staffing for key enforcement occupations declined to 20,722 from 21,187 in FY2007; the percentage of individual tax returns examined fell to 1.01%; and the percentage of business tax returns examined decreased to 0.63%.[26] For FY2008, the IRS reported a reduction in enforcement revenues to $56.4 billion from $59.2 billion in FY2007.[27] For FY2009, IRS

---

[23] Ibid.

[24] U.S. Department of the Treasury, Internal Revenue Service, *Fiscal Year 2011 Enforcement Results*, p. 1.

[25] Ibid., pp. 2-6.

[26] Ibid., pp. 1-4.

[27] **Appendix B** contains data on IRS enforcement revenues collected and staffing for key enforcement occupations for (continued...)

---

appropriations rose to $11.5 billion and enforcement funding rose to $5.1 billion.[28] For FY2009, staffing for key enforcement occupations rose to 21,059, but enforcement revenue collected declined sharply to $48.9 billion.[29] This amount of revenue collected is only $0.2 billion above the amount collected in FY2006. Mr. Steve Miller, the deputy commissioner for services and enforcement, reportedly said that this decline in revenue collected between FY2008 and FY2009 was due to two factors: the recession and the closing of a significant number of high-grossing tax shelter cases, namely those regarding "Son of Boss" (bond option sales strategy) transactions.[30] The closing of Son of Boss cases also caused a spike in enforcement revenues in FY2007 compared to FY2006.[31] The IRS describes Son of Boss transactions as arrangements that are "designed to produce noneconomic tax losses on the disposition of partnership interests."[32] For FY2010, enforcement revenue collected rebounded to $57.6 billion but declined to $55.2 billion in FY2011. IRS enforcement staffing was 22,710 in FY2010 and 22,184 in FY2011. Taken together those observations suggest that enforcement alone will not effectively close the tax gap.

As a result, rather than focusing only on enforcement, the Treasury Department and the Government Accountability Office (GAO)[33] argued that a comprehensive strategy was needed to reduce the tax gap.

Comprehensive Strategy for Reducing the Tax Gap

The Office of Tax Policy at the Treasury developed what it considered a comprehensive strategy for reducing the tax gap, guided by the following four key principles:[34]

- Unintentional taxpayer errors and intentional taxpayer evasion should both be addressed.

- Sources of noncompliance should be targeted with specificity.

- Enforcement activities should be combined with a commitment to taxpayer service.

(...continued)

FY2001-FY2011.

[28] Office of Management and Budget, *Budget of the U.S. Government, Fiscal Year 2011* (Washington: GPO, 2010), p. 115.

[29] U.S. Treasury, Internal Revenue Service, *Fiscal Year 2011 Enforcement Results*, p. 1.

[30] Lauren Gardner, "IRS FY 2009 Enforcement Data Show Impact of Drop in Enforcement Revenue," *Daily Tax Report*, no. 244, December 23, 2009, p. G5.

[31] Ibid.

[32] U.S. Department of the Treasury, Treasury Inspector General for Tax Administration, *Despite the Success Achieved, the Son of Boss Settlement Had Little Impact on Investor Filing and Payment Compliance*, reference number 2009-30-018, December 30, 2008, p. 1.

[33] U.S. Government Accountability Office, *Tax Compliance: Multiple Approaches Are Needed to Reduce the Tax Gap*, Statement of Michael Brostek, Director, Tax Issues Strategic Issues Team, before U.S. Congress, Senate Committee on the Budget, January 23, 2007.

[34] U.S. Department of the Treasury, Office of Tax Policy, *A Comprehensive Strategy for Reducing the Tax Gap*, September 26, 2006. This report was updated with more detailed information about the tax gap and components of the strategy to reduce the tax gap. This updated report is U.S. Department of the Treasury, Internal Revenue Service, *Reducing the Federal Tax Gap, Report on Improving Voluntary Compliance*, August 2, 2007. On July 8, 2009, a second update was issued by the U.S. Treasury, *Update on Reducing the Federal Tax Gap and Improving Voluntary Compliance*.

- Policy positions and compliance proposals should be sensitive to taxpayer rights and maintain an appropriate balance between enforcement activity and imposition of taxpayer burden.[35]

Over time, the strategic focus on reducing the tax gap evolved into a broader array of IRS priorities.

IRS Strategic Priorities

On April 5, 2012, at the National Press Club, IRS Commissioner Douglas H. Shulman explained the six strategy priorities that had been a relentless focus of the IRS over the preceding four years.[36] The IRS's pursuit of most of these priorities reduced the tax gap.

- **Creating New Capabilities and Efficiencies Through Technology**

Since the 1960s, the IRS had conducted its core account processing on a weekly basis. This processing included basic taxpayer information, such as a taxpayer's current account balance, whether the taxpayer had an outstanding amounts due, and whether the taxpayer made any recent payments. This year the IRS successfully migrated from a weekly processing cycle to daily processing.

The payoffs from this change are quicker tax return processing for all taxpayers, up-to-date information at the fingertips of IRS's customer account representatives, and a platform for more real-time analytics and compliance.

- **Rethinking and Reimagining the IRS's Relationship with Paid Tax Return Preparers**

In 2011, 95 million individual and business income tax returns were prepared by paid preparers. The IRS is now well into the process of ensuring a basic competency level for tax return preparers and focusing our enforcement efforts on rooting out unscrupulous preparers. The IRS has registered over 840,000 return preparers and has begun administering a competency test for any preparer who is not a CPA, attorney, or enrolled agent. These individuals also have to complete 15 hours of continuing education each year from IRS-approved providers.[37]

- **Leveraging Data Analytics for Continuous Improvement**

This IRS has always been an information intensive enterprise. But what matters is the organization of data and ultimately the knowledge and intelligence that IRS extracts from the information. The IRS built a team of people with analytical expertise and connected them with its business units to improve operations continually. They are working on multiple fronts, and the results have been significant.

---

[35] U.S. Department of the Treasury, Office of Tax Policy, *A Comprehensive Strategy for Reducing the Tax Gap*, pp. 1-2.

[36] U.S. Department of the Treasury, Internal Revenue Service, News Release (IR-2012-42), *Prepared Remarks of Commissioner of Internal Revenue*, April 15, 2012. The following six bulleted entries are a mix of direct or slightly edited quotes from his prepared remarks.

[37] This initiative is examined in detail in the next section of this report.

For example, using better data on return preparers that was gained through IRS's return preparer initiatives and faster processing cycles, the IRS applied advanced data analytics to link tax returns that showed potentially serious compliance issues to the individuals who prepared them. The IRS identified a number of preparers with apparently inaccurate returns and, depending on the type and severity of the issue, is applying different types of compliance tools.

- **Enhancing Taxpayer Service Capabilities**

Providing quality customer service is a key priority of the IRS. Every year the American Customer Satisfaction Index measures customer satisfaction across various industries and government agencies. This composite index is the main measure used by the IRS to track its overall performance. For 1998, only 32% of respondents voiced satisfaction with IRS service, but this percentage rose to 73% in 2011.

Two examples of IRS innovations to improve customer service were e-filing and IRS's Smartphone application called "IRS2Go." In 2011, 77% of individuals used e-filing, which resulted in taxpayers receiving their refunds faster, with fewer data processing errors. The IRS Smartphone application permits taxpayers to check on the status of their refund and obtain other helpful tax information on their iPhones or Androids.

- **Transforming the Agency to Confront the Challenges of a Global Economy**

In a world where products are routinely sold after intellectual property is generated in one or more countries ... where logistics and engineering are carried out in other counties ... where risks are managed in a variety of places ... and where components are sourced from multiple jurisdictions, figuring out what U.S. corporate income tax may be appropriate when the products go to market can be a challenge to say the least.

For individuals, the IRS views the reduction of offshore tax evasion as an issue of fundamental fairness. Over the past four years, the IRS significantly increased its resources and focus on offshore tax evasion, and the results have been substantial. In 2009, the IRS gave taxpayers, involved in offshore tax evasion, a chance to come in voluntarily and avoid going to jail. At the end of 2011, approximately 33,000 individuals had voluntarily disclosed their unpaid offshore taxes, and consequently, paid more than $4.4 billion in back taxes and penalties.

The IRS is moving from information sharing to more coordinated action among government tax authorities on a global basis. The Commissioner of the IRS is the chairman of the main global body of tax authorities, which comprises his counterparts from 43 nations, including those from all G20 nations.[38]

- **Positioning the IRS Workforce to Prepare for Tomorrow's Challenges**

The IRS initiated the "Workforce of Tomorrow Task Force" with the stated purpose objective of making the IRS the best place to work in government. The IRS put an emphasis on key

---

[38] The G20 includes 19 country members and the European Union, which together represent around 90% of Global GDP, 80% of global trade, and two-thirds of the world's population. The G20 is a forum for international cooperation on important aspects of the international economic and financial agenda. This description is from the following G20 website: http://www.g20.org/index.php/en/what-is-the-g20.

factors including engagement, accountability, career paths, and management to position the agency for excellence in the future. From 2008 to 2011, the IRS jumped from eighth to third place among the fifteen large agencies with over 20,000 employees in the survey of the "Best Place to Work in the Federal Government."

Following IRS Commissioner Shulman's annual speech, much of the question-and- answer period focused on IRS's return preparer initiative.[39]

IRS Return Preparer Initiative

In June 2009, the IRS began a review of tax return preparers and obtained extensive feedback from a diverse community of stakeholders.[40] The IRS had the authority to establish regulations regarding tax return preparers without legislative approval. After a review of return preparers, the IRS established a return preparer initiative with new regulations, which it began implementing in 2010.[41]

On June 5, 2012, the IRS marked the third anniversary of it return preparer initiative and indicated that major facets of the initiative were now in place.[42] The IRS published the following initiative highlights:[43]

- **Mandatory Registration and Use of a Preparer Tax Identification Number (PTIN):** Anyone who is paid to prepare, or help prepare, all or substantially all of a federal tax return now has to register with the IRS and obtain a PTIN, as do all enrolled agents. The PTIN is valid for a calendar year and must be renewed annually. Almost 850,000 preparers have registered since the requirement began.

- **Competency Test:** In November 2011, a 120-question basic competency test was launched. Certain preparers are required to take the test by December 31, 2013, to stay in business. The IRS urges an estimated 340,000 preparers required to take the test to do so as soon as possible to give themselves more time if they have to retake the test and to avoid a potential flood of last-minute test takers. Certified Public Accountants (CPAs), Enrolled Agents (EAs), and attorneys are exempt from the test because they already have other testing requirements as part of their credentials. Certain non-signing preparers supervised by CPAs, EAs, or attorneys are exempt, as are non-1040 preparers.

- **Continuing Education (CE):** The roughly 340,000 preparers who have a testing requirement also have a new requirement to complete 15 hours of continuing education courses each year. The CE credits must include 10 hours in federal tax

---

[39] Rachel Boehm, "Shulman to Step Down in November; IRS Priorities Include Extenders, Preparers," *Daily Tax Report*, April 6, 2012, p. G2.

[40] U.S. Department of the Treasury, Internal Revenue Service, *Return Preparer Review*, Publication 4832, December 2009, p. 1.

[41] Ibid., pp. 3-5.

[42] U.S. Department of the Treasury, Internal Revenue Service, "IRS Marks Third Anniversary of Return Preparer Review; Urges Required Preparers to Take Competency Test as Soon as Possible," IRS New Release (IR-2012-59), June 5, 2012, p. 1.

[43] The following bulleted entries are mix of direct or slightly edited quotes from U.S. Department of the Treasury, Internal Revenue Service, "IRS Marks Third Anniversary of Return Preparer Review," pp. 1-2.

law, three hours in federal tax law changes, and two hours in ethics. This requirement became effective January 2012 and it applies even if the preparer has not yet taken the test. There are now hundreds of outlets offering IRS-approved CE courses. More details are available at http://www.irs.gov/taxpros/ce.

- **Ethics and Tax Compliance:** Ethical requirements that previously applied only to CPAs, EAs, and attorneys now apply to all paid return preparers. All paid preparers also will undergo a tax compliance check and are subject to the standards for practice outlined in Treasury Department Circular 230.

- **Registered Tax Return Preparer (RTRP):** Preparers who pass the competency test and tax compliance check are given a new credential: Registered Tax Return Preparer. To date, over 4,800 people have become Registered Tax Return Preparers. Beginning in 2014, only Registered Tax Return Preparers, Enrolled Agents, Certified Public Accountants, and attorneys will be authorized to prepare individual income tax returns for compensation.

- **Public Database:** The IRS also will create a publicly searchable database that will allow taxpayers to see if their tax preparers have met IRS standards or to find a tax preparer in their zip code area. The IRS will have a public education campaign to inform taxpayers to use only CPAs, EAs, attorneys, or Registered Tax Return Preparers if they pay to have their taxes prepared. The database will also show any credentials held by the preparer, including the new RTRP credential, as well as those who are EAs, CPAs, and attorneys. The RTRP competency test is available at more than 260 vendor testing centers nationwide. Preparers can determine if they have a test requirement by going to their online PTIN Account at http://www.irs.gov/tin. Preparers also can set a test date, time and location through their online PTIN Account.

Proposed Legislation in the 112th Congress

In the 112th Congress, numerous bills have been proposed concerning the tax gap and tax compliance. All of these bills were referred to committee, and one has become public law. These bills are categorized into seven categories and described in the following sections.[44]

Repeal of 1099 Reporting Requirement

P.L. 112-9, (H.R. 4). Comprehensive 1099 Taxpayer Protection and Repayment of Exchange Subsidy Overpayments Act of 2011

On January 12, 2011, Representative Daniel E. Lungren introduced H.R. 4. On April 14, 2011, this bill became P.L. 112-9. Because the bill was enacted, the related bills (H.Res. 129, H.R. 60, H.R. 144, H.R. 584, H.R. 705, S. 18, S. 72, S. 359) are not described in this report.

---

[44] Unless indicated otherwise, these descriptions are quotes or paraphrases from the CRS Legislative Information System data base.

This public law amended the Internal Revenue Code to (1) repeal requirements for the reporting to the IRS of payments of $600 or more to corporations that are not tax-exempt and of gross proceeds of $600 or more paid in consideration for any type of property; (2) repeal requirements for reporting payments made with respect to rental property which is not part of a trade or business; and (3) increase, for taxable years ending after December 31, 2013, the advance applicable dollar amount of the tax credit for health care premium assistance for taxpayers whose household income is less the 400% of the poverty line.[45]

Identity Theft

Five bills were introduced concerning identify theft: H.R. 3215, H.R. 3338, H.R. 3482, H.R. 6205, S. 1534, and S. 3432.

S. 1534, S. 3432, and H.R. 3215—Identify Theft and Tax Fraud Prevention Act

On September 8, 2011, Senator Bill Nelson introduced S. 1534. On July 25, 2012, Senator Nelson introduced S. 3432. On October 14, 2011, Representative Kathy Castor introduced H.R. 3215. S. 1534, S. 3432, and H.R. 3215 are related bills.

The bills would amend the Internal Revenue Code to (1) impose a fine and/or prison term on any person who knowingly or willfully misappropriates another person's tax identification number in connection with any list, return, account, statement, or other documents submitted to the IRS; (2) increase the civil and criminal penalties for improper disclosure or use of taxpayer information by tax return preparers; (3) require the Commissioner of Internal Revenue to submit to the Senate Committee on Finance and the House Committee on Ways and Means an annual report on the number of reported cases of tax fraud and suspected tax fraud and the actions taken in response to such reports; and (4) require the head of the Federal Bureau of Prisons to submit to Congress a detailed plan on how it will use tax information provided by the IRS to reduce prison tax fraud.

The bills would direct the Secretary of the Treasury to (1) implement an identity theft tax fraud prevention program; and (2) review whether current federal tax law prevents the effective enforcement of local, state, and federal identity theft statutes.

The bills would authorize the IRS Commissioner to transfer appropriated funds to be used solely to prevent and resolve potential tax fraud cases.

The bills would direct the Commissioner to establish in the Criminal Investigation Division of the IRS the position of Local Law Enforcement Liaison to coordinate the investigation of tax fraud with state and local law enforcement agencies and communicate the status of tax fraud cases involving identity theft.

The bills would direct the Comptroller General to study and report on the role of prepaid debit cards and commercial tax preparation software in facilitating fraudulent tax returns through identity theft.

---

[45] For more information, see CRS Report R41782, *1099 Information Reporting Requirements and Penalties: Recent Legislative Activity*, by Carol A. Pettit and Edward C. Liu.

The bills would prohibit the Secretary of Commerce from disclosing information contained in the Death Master File relating to deceased individual to persons who are not certified to access such information.[46]

S. 3432 differs from the other two bills in that it includes a section titled "Prohibiting the Display of Social Security Account Numbers on Newly Issued Medicare Identification Cards and Communications Provided to Medicare Beneficiaries."

H.R. 3482—Tax Crimes and Identity Theft Prevention Act

On December 2, 2011, Representative Kathy Castor introduced H.R. 3482, which is related to S. 1534 and H.R. 3215. The only addition to the preceding summary on S. 1534/S. 3215 is a section that authorizes the Attorney General to award grants to state and local law enforcement agencies for the investigation and prosecution of tax crimes.

H.R. 6205—Protect and Save Act of 2012

On July 26, 2012, Representative Richard Nugent introduced H.R. 6205.[47]

The bill would authorize the Secretary of the Treasury to disclose income tax return information to officers and employees of any federal law enforcement agency, or any officers and employees of any state or local law enforcement agency, who are personally and directly engaged in the investigation of any crimes pertaining to the misuse of the identity of another person for purposes of filing a false or fraudulent tax return, upon receipt of a written request. This request must be made by the head of the agency (or his delegate) involved in the investigation, and the request must set forth the specific reason why such disclosure may be relevant to the investigation.

The bill would require the Commissioner of the IRS to establish within the Criminal Investigation Division the position of Local Law Enforcement Liaison. The bill would also require the Secretary of the Treasury (or the Secretary's delegate) to implement an identify theft fraud prevention program.

The bill would require the Comptroller General to conduct a study on the use of prepaid debit cards and commercial tax preparation software in tax fraud. The bill would also require the Comptroller General to study the use of e-filing in tax fraud. The bill would extend the authority of the IRS to disclose certain tax return information to prison officials.

The bill would restrict the Secretary of Commerce in disclosing information contained in the Social Security Death Master File with respect to any individual who had died during the previous two calendar years.

---

[46] The Social Security Death Master File is a database used by leading government, financial investigative, and credit reporting organizations and medical research and other industries to verify death as well as to prevent fraud. This information is from the U.S. Department of Commerce, National Technical Information Service, at http://www.ntis.gov/products/ssa-dmf.aspx.

[47] This description was written by the author.

Free File

S. 1796 and H.R. 2569—Free File Program Act of 2011

On November 3, 2011, Senator Mark L. Pryor introduced S. 1796. On July 15, 2011, Representative Peter J. Roskam introduced H.R. 2569. S. 1796 and H.R. 2569 are related bills.

These bills authorize and direct the Secretary of the Treasury to continue to implement and operate the Internal Revenue Service's Free File program (free online individual income tax preparation and electronic filing services provided by the private sector technology industry to lower-income taxpayers).

Contracting

H.R. 829—Contracting and Tax Accountability Act of 2011

On February 28, 2011, Representative Jason Chaffetz introduced H.R. 829.

This bill would prohibit any person who has a seriously delinquent tax debt from obtaining a federal government contract or grant. The bill would require federal agency heads to require prospective recipients of a contract or grant in excess of an amount equal to the simplified acquisition threshold to (1) certify that they do not have such a debt; and (2) authorize the Secretary of the Treasury to disclose information describing whether they have such a debt.

The bill would define "seriously delinquent tax debt" as an outstanding tax debt for which a notice of lien has been filed in public records.

Insurance Companies

S. 1693 and H.R. 3157—A Bill to Amend the Internal Revenue Code of 1986 to Prevent the Avoidance of Tax by Insurance Companies through Reinsurance with Non-taxed Affiliates

On October 12, 2011, Senator Robert Menendez introduced S. 1693. On October 12, 2011, Representative Richard E. Neal introduced H.S. 3157. S. 1693 and H.R. 3157 are related bills.

These bills would amend the Internal Revenue Code to exclude from the taxable income of a life insurance company or other insurance company (1) any non-taxed reinsurance premium; (2) any additional amount paid by an insurance company with respect to the reinsurance for which such non-taxed reinsurance premium is paid; and (3) any return premium, ceding commission, reinsurance recovered, or other amount received by an insurance company with respect to the reinsurance for which such non-taxed reinsurance premium is paid.

Tax Havens[48]

In the 112ᵗʰ Congress, four bills concerning tax havens have been introduced: S. 1346, H.R. 2669, H.R. 3338, and S. 2075.

S. 1346 and H.R. 2669—Stop Tax Haven Abuse Act

On July 12, 2011, Senator Carl Levin introduced S. 1346. On July 27, 2011, Representative Lloyd Doggett introduced H.R. 2669. S. 1346 and H.R. 2699 are related bills.

These bills would authorize the Secretary of the Treasury to impose restrictions on foreign jurisdictions or financial institutions operating in the United States that are of prime money laundering concern or that impede U.S. tax enforcement.

The bills would amend the Internal Revenue Code to (1) establish a rebuttable presumption against the validity of transactions by institutions that do not comply with reporting requirements under the Foreign Account Tax Compliance Act (FATCA); (2) treat certain foreign corporations managed and controlled primarily in the United States as domestic corporations for tax purposes; (3) require tax withholding agents and financial institutions to report certain information about beneficial owners of foreign-owned financial accounts; (4) treat credit default swap payments sent offshore as taxable U.S. source income; (5) allow the use of tax return information to evaluate foreign financial account reports; (6) increase penalties for promoting abusive tax shelters and for aiding and abetting the understatement of tax liability; (7) prohibit tax advisor contingent fee agreements for obtaining a tax savings or benefit; and (8) impose additional requirements for third-party summonses used to obtain information in tax investigations that do not identify the person with respect to whose liability the summons is issued.

The bills would amend the Securities Exchange Act of 1934 to (1) require corporations registered with the Securities and Exchange Commission (SEC) to report annually, on a country-by-country basis, on employees' sales, financing, tax obligations, and tax payments; and (2) authorize a fine of up to $1 million for failure to disclose any holding or transaction involving equity or debt instruments known to involve a foreign entity that would otherwise be subject to disclosure requirements.

The bills would require the Treasury Secretary to publish a proposed rule in the *Federal Register* requiring unregistered investment companies, including hedge funds or private equity funds, to establish anti-money laundering programs and submit suspicious activity reports.

The bills would extend anti-money laundering requirements to persons engaged in the business of forming new businesses or other legal entities.

The bills would require federal banking agencies and the SEC to develop examination techniques to detect and prevent abusive tax shelter activities or the aiding or abetting of tax evasion by financial institutions.

---

[48] For an analysis of tax havens, see CRS Report R40623, *Tax Havens: International Tax Avoidance and Evasion*, by Jane G. Gravelle.

The bills would require the Treasury Secretary to (1) disclose tax return information to federal financial regulators for purposes of tax-shelter investigations; (2) disclose to Congress documents relating to a determination to grant, deny, revoke, or restore the tax-exempt status of an organization; and (3) expand the standards applicable to tax practitioners for issuing written advice on transactions which have a potential for tax avoidance or evasion.

S. 2075 — CUT Loopholes Act or Cut Unjustified Tax Loopholes Act

On February 7, 2012, Senator Carl Levin introduced S. 2075, which is related to S. 1346 and H.R. 2669. The significant difference is that S. 2075 would curtail tax advantages for stock options.[49]

H.R. 3338 — Stop Outsourcing and Create American Jobs Act of 2011

On November 3, 2011, Representative Jerry McNerney introduced H.R. 3338.

The bill would direct the Secretary of the Treasury to develop and publish a list of countries that are tax havens for corporations.

The bill would amend the Internal Revenue Code to increase the penalties on corporations for (1) underpayment of tax involving an undisclosed foreign asset located in a tax-haven country; (2) reportable transaction understatements involving transactions in a tax-haven country; and (3) fraud, tax evasion, or false statements involving transactions in a tax-haven country.

The bill would require revenues generated by the act to be set aside for the reduction of the public debt.

Tax Avoidance by Expatriates

S. 3205 — Ex-PATRIOT Act or Expatriation Prevention by Abolishing Tax-Related Incentives for Offshore Tenancy Act

On May 17, 2012, Senator Charles E. Schumer introduced S. 3205.

This bill would amend the Internal Revenue Code to impose a 30% tax and withholding on capital gains income realized by a nonresident alien individual present in the United States for periods aggregating to 183 days or more or an expatriate who has renounced his or her U.S. citizenship for tax avoidance purposes (specified expatriate).

This bill would amend the Immigration and Nationality Act to (1) render a specified expatriate inadmissible to the United State; and (2) prohibit any waiver of such inadmissibility. The bill would direct the Secretary of the Treasury, in consultation with the Secretaries of State and Homeland Security, to develop a policy for granting a waiver of inadmissibility to a specified expatriate who satisfies a tax liability related to such expatriate's renunciation of U.S. citizenship.

---

[49] For an explanation of the taxation of employee stock options, see CRS Report RL31458, *Employee Stock Options: Tax Treatment and Tax Issues*, by James M. Bickley.

Appendix A. Tax Gap Data for 2006

Figure A-1. Tax Year 2006

Tax Year 2006 ($ billions)

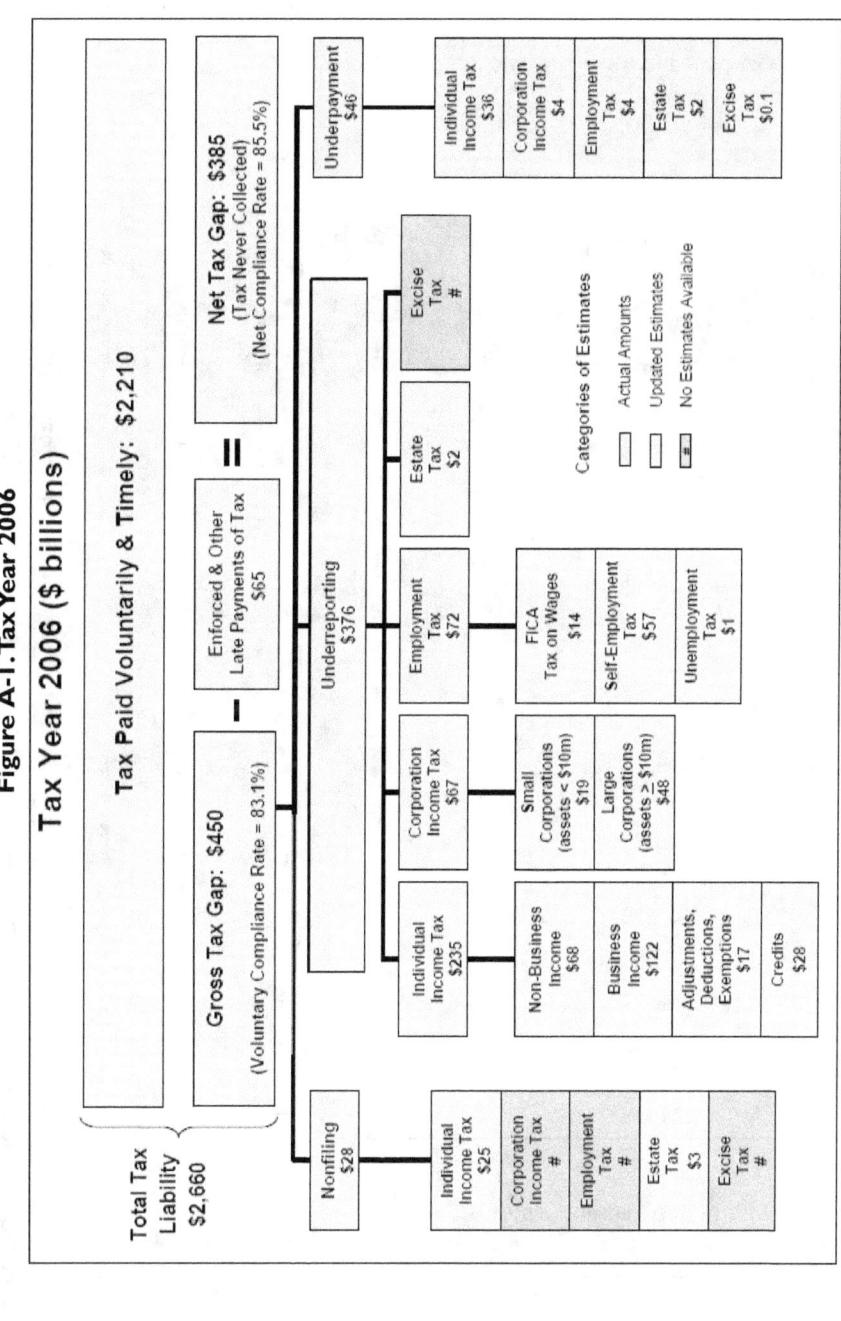

Source: U.S. Treasury, Internal Revenue Service, December 2011.

Figure A-2. Effect of Information Reporting on Taxpayer Compliance, 2006

Tax Year 2006 Individual Income Tax Underreporting Gap and Net Misreporting Percentage, by "Visibility" Category

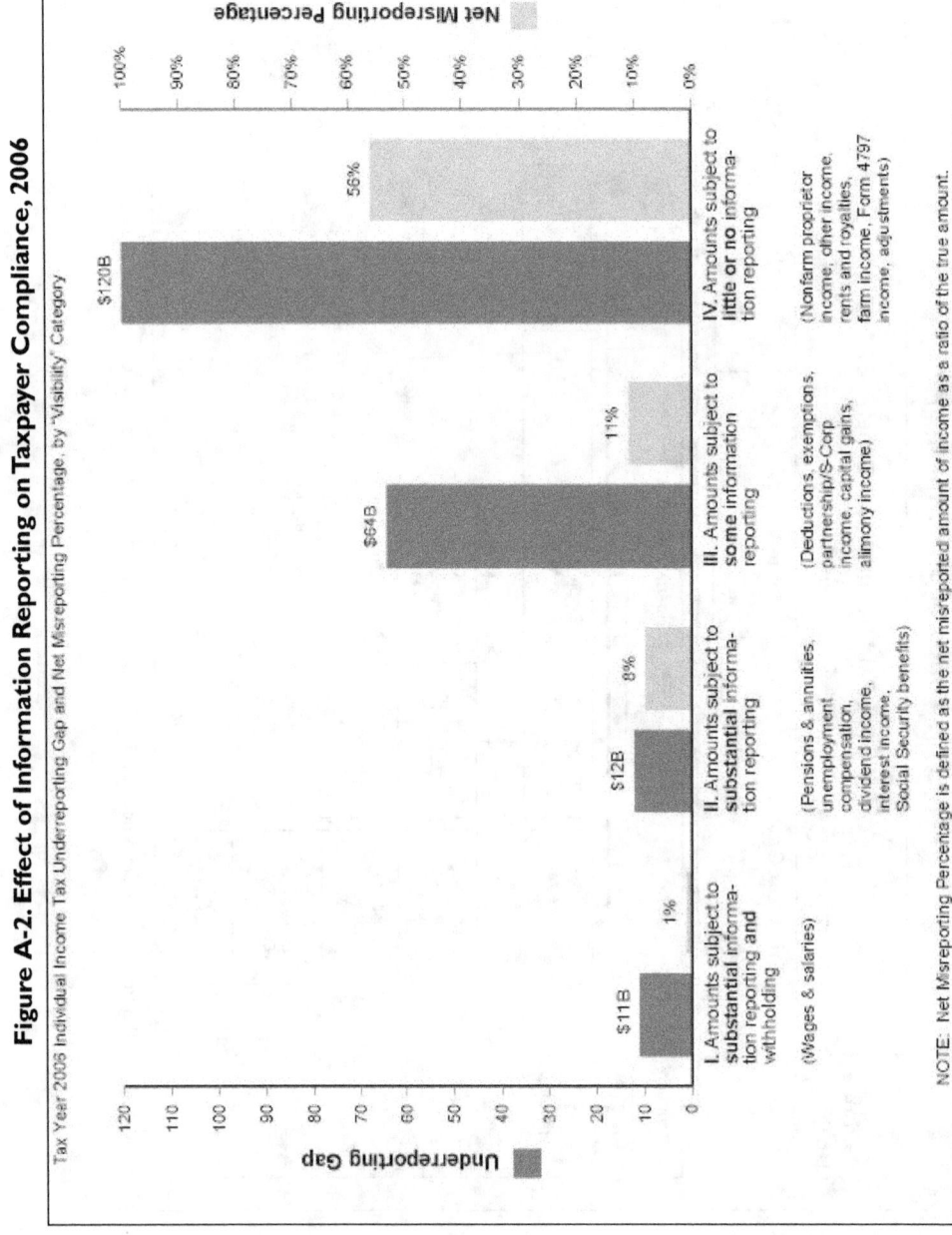

NOTE: Net Misreporting Percentage is defined as the net misreported amount of income as a ratio of the true amount.

Source: U.S. Treasury, Internal Revenue Service, December 2011.

Appendix B. IRS Enforcement Results

Table B-1. Enforcement Revenues Collected, FY2001-FY2011

(billions of dollars)

	FY2001	FY2002	FY2003	FY2004	FY2005	FY2006	FY2007	FY2008	FY2009	FY2010	FY2011
Collection[a]	$24.3	$24.4	$24.8	$25.7	$26.6	$28.2	$31.8	$31.1	$26.9	$29.1	$31.1
Examination	$7.9	$7.9	$10.7	$14.7	$17.7	$17.2	$23.5	$20.6	$17.4	$16.9	$12.4
Appeals[b]	$2.3	$2.2	$1.9	$2.2	$3.9	$4.3	$8.3	$4.8	$4.8	$6.7	$6.5
Documentation Matching	$1.6	$1.8	$2.2	$2.7	$3.1	$3.3	$3.9	$4.7	$4.6	$4.9	$5.2
Total[c]	**$33.8**	**$34.1**	**$37.6**	**$43.1**	**$47.3**	**$48.7**	**$59.2**	**$56.4**	**$48.9**	**$57.6**	**$55.2**

Source: U.S. Department of the Treasury, Internal Revenue Service, 2011.

a. Enforcement revenue collected in a fiscal year includes tax, interest, and penalties from multiple years.

b. Includes any revenue collection attributable to IRS appeals activities.

c. Totals include revenues from the Information Reporter Program (IRP) and the Automated Underreporter (AUR) Program.

Table B-2. Staffing for Key Enforcement Occupations, FY2001-FY2011

	FY2001	FY2002	FY2003	FY2004	FY2005	FY2006	FY2007	FY2008	FY2009	FY2010	FY2011
Revenue Officers[a]	5,376	5,502	5,076	5,156	5,249	5,627	5,662	5,492	5,451	6,042	5,619
Revenue Agents	12,092	11,743	11,780	11,811	12,192	12,778	12,816	12,599	12,958	13,888	13,867
Special Agents	2,735	2,868	2,834	2,778	2,771	2,780	2,709	2,631	2,650	2,780	2,698
Total	**20,203**	**20,113**	**19,691**	**19,746**	**20,211**	**21,185**	**21,187**	**20,722**	**21,059**	**22,710**	**22,184**

Source: U.S. Department of the Treasury, Internal Revenue Service, 2011.

a. Enforcement staffing levels presented in full time equivalents (FTEs). FTEs funded directly by the enforcement appropriation and by reimbursements are included.

Author Contact Information

James M. Bickley
Specialist in Public Finance
jbickley@crs.loc.gov, 7-7794